Praying Mantises

Edited by Heather C. Hudak

Published by Weigl Publishers Inc.
350 5th Avenue, Suite 3304, PMB 6G
New York, NY 10118-0069
Website: www.weigl.com

Library of Congress Cataloging-in-Publication Data

Praying mantises : world of wonder / edited by Heather C. Hudak.
    p. cm.
 Includes index.
 ISBN 978-1-59036-872-5 (hard cover : alk. paper) -- ISBN 978-1-59036-873-2 (soft cover : alk. paper)
 1. Praying mantis--Juvenile literature. I. Hudak, Heather C., 1975-
 QL505.9.M35P73 2009
 595.7'27--dc22

                    2008023854

Printed in the United States of America
1 2 3 4 5 6 7 8 9 0 12 11 10 09 08

Editor: Heather C. Hudak
Design: Terry Paulhus

Weigl acknowledges Getty Images as one of its primary image suppliers for this title.

CONTENTS

What is a Praying Mantis?

Have you ever seen an insect that looks like it is praying? This may have been a praying mantis.

A praying mantis is a type of insect. There are about 2,000 types of mantis in the world.

Female mantises are among the biggest insects on Earth.

5

Back in Time

Could you imagine living at the time of the dinosaurs? The remains of an ancient praying mantis were found in Japan. This mantis dates back about 87 million years!

Praying mantises first came to North America in 1895 with a shipment of plants from China. Today, these insects are found from coast to coast.

Praying Mantis Life Cycle

What if you had hundreds of brothers and sisters? The female praying mantis lays groups of 12 to 400 eggs in a **frothy** liquid. This liquid is called *ootheca*. It hardens into a shell around the eggs.

Young mantises hatch from the eggs in spring. They shed their skin many times before becoming full grown. It takes an entire summer season for a mantis to grow into an adult.

Preparing to lay eggs

Ootheca

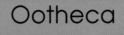

Young mantis

Adult mantis

What Does a Praying Mantis Look Like?

How many body parts do you have? Praying mantises have six legs, a pair of **antennae**, a head, thorax, and abdomen.

A mantis's front legs are used for grabbing and holding **prey**. Its other legs are used for walking, climbing, and jumping. Mantises have two, large, round eyes. They can move their eyes freely to see all around them.

head

thorax

abdomen

Master of Disguise

What if you could blend in with the toys and clothes in your bedroom? Praying mantises blend into their **habitat**.

Mantises are the same color and shape as the plants they live on. This is so that **predators** cannot find them easily. It also helps them stay hidden from prey.

To most people, mantises look like twigs or leaves.

Look, I Have Wings!

Imagine if you had wings. Would you use them to fly? Praying mantises have two sets of wings. They use their wings to scare away predators, such as birds.

Praying mantises fan their brightly colored wings when they see a predator. This makes the mantis look much larger. Some mantises have spots on their wings. These spots look like angry eyes.

What's for Dinner?

Do you eat your meals with a fork or spoon? Praying mantises use spikes on their front legs to grab prey.

Praying mantises mostly eat insects. They also eat small tree frogs, lizards, mice, and hummingbirds.

While searching for food, mantises hide in plant stems. When prey passes by, the mantis grabs it.

Before striking their prey, mantises rock back and forth. Some people believe mantises look like leaves in the wind. Others think this helps mantises focus their eyesight.

Home Sweet Home

Praying mantises live in warm environments throughout the world. They live in forests, parks, fields, and gardens where there are many plants. These places must have plenty of other insects and animals for the mantises to eat.

Insect Lore

There are many stories about praying mantises around the world. In France, some people believe that a praying mantis can help a person who is lost find his or her way home.

In Africa, when a praying mantis lands on a person, it is said to bring good luck.

Some people believe that praying mantises kneel when angels are nearby.

Draw a Praying Mantis

Supplies
Crayons or colored pencils, a pencil, a sheet of paper

1. Draw a triangle on a sheet of paper.

2. Below the triangle, draw a long rectangle.

3. Below the rectangle, draw a thin oval.

4. Add lines to make legs and antennae.

5. Use crayons or colored pencils to color your drawing.

Find Out More

To learn more about praying mantises, visit these websites.

Insecta Inspecta World
www.insecta-inspecta.com/
mantids/praying/index.html

Praying Mantis
www.enchantedlearning.com
/subjects/insects/mantids/
Prayingmantidprintout.html

WonderClub.com
www.wonderclub.com/
Wildlife/insectsandspiders/
praying_mantis.htm

Praying Mantid Information

Return to previous page
Phylum, Arthropoda; **Class**, Insecta; **Order**, Mantodea

Identifying Features

Appearance (Morphology)

- Three distinct body regions: head, thorax (where the legs and wings are attached), abdomen.
- Part of the thorax is elongated to create a distinctive 'neck'.
- Front legs modified as raptorial graspers with strong spikes for grabbing and holding prey.
- Large compound eyes on the head which moves freely around (up to 180°) and three simple eyes between the compound eyes.
- Incomplete or simple metamorphosis (hemimetabolous).

Female praying mantid with front legs poised for capturing prey.

Adult Males and Females
Females usually have heavier abdomen and are larger than males.

Immatures (different stages)
A distinct Styrofoam-like egg case protects Mantid eggs throughout the winter. Up to 200 or more nymphs may emerge from the egg case. The nymphs look like adults except for size and the sexual definition. Coloration and patterns in the nymph stage may be different than the adult.

Natural History

Food
Praying mantids are highly predacious and feed on a variety of insects, including moths, crickets, grasshoppers and flies. They lie in wait with the front legs in an upraised position. They intently watch and stalk their prey. They will eat each other.

Habitat
Praying mantids are often protectively colored to the plants they live on. This camouflage facilitates their predaceous behavior. Mantids are usually found on plants that have other insects around. Some mantids live in grass. Winged adults may be attracted to black lights in late summer and early fall.

Predators
Many fish and predatory aquatic insects eat larvae and pupae. Bats, birds and spiders eat flying adults.

Interesting Behaviors
The adult female usually eats the male after or during mating. Mantid's

FEATURE SITE:
http://insected.arizona.edu/
mantidinfo.htm

Glossary

antennae: long, thin body parts that extend from an insect's head

frothy: foamy

habitat: natural environments of living things

predators: animals that hunt other animals for food

prey: animals that are hunted by other animals for food

Index